An opin

LONDON MARKETS

Written by
SONYA BARBER

Photography by
CHANEL IRVINE

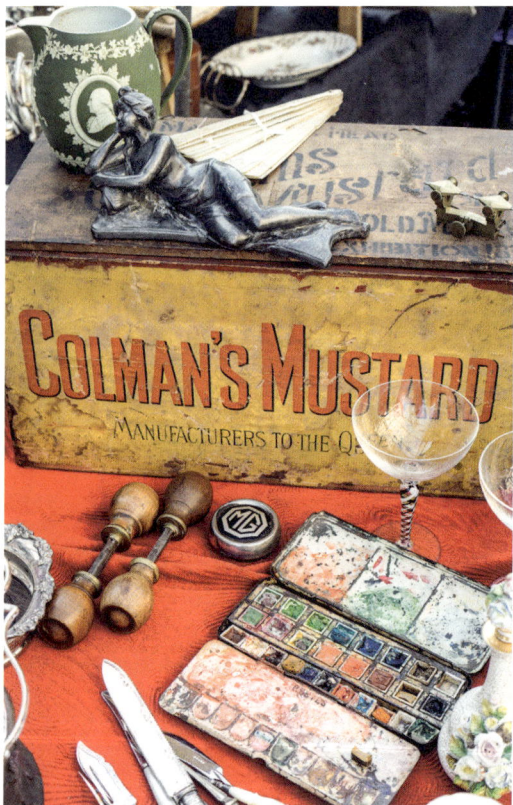

Bermondsey Antique Market (no.20)

INFORMATION IS DEAD.
LONG LIVE OPINION.

Why buy a guide book when you can simply Google – sorry, ChatGPT (is that a verb?) – all you need to know about London markets? Well, for the same reason you don't want a robot to search out a second-hand watch or find you the freshest bagel. You go to a market to be visually delighted, to hear unexpected voices, to be surprised and informed. This book is made by humans, with real opinions, telling you which of London's markets are the best and exactly why. Rummage through these pages, then rummage for some treasures in the real world. Enjoy.

Martin
Hoxton Mini Press

WHELOK
£6.50 og

oyster
£1
cah

New Covent Garden Market (no.32)
Opposite: Chapel Market (no.43)

Columbia Road Flower Market (no.1)
Opposite: Parliament Hill Farmers' Market (no.44)

WILD COUNTRY
ORGANICS
ORGANIC VEGETABLES

Bermondsey Antique Market (no.20)
Opposite: Grays Antique Market (no.37)

THIS LITTLE PIGGY
WENT TO MARKET...

London is built on markets. As long ago as 70 AD, the forum of Roman London (roughly where Leadenhall Market is today) was Europe's largest marketplace, bringing toga-wearing Londoners together to meet and shop.

Over the last 20 centuries, London's markets have proliferated, selling vegetables, cattle, fish and flowers, and servicing the growing suburbs. Some of the city's most famous neighbourhoods – like Peckham, Camberwell, Brixton and Fulham – were first developed as market gardens, growing veggies for the big markets of central London. Many more areas flourished around local markets, which were (and still are) a haven for migrant groups to meet up and buy foods from home. A surprising number of these historic marketplaces are still going strong: there have been markets at Greenwich and Borough since the 12th century, Brick Lane since the 17th century and Portobello and Billingsgate since the early 19th century.

Today, markets are still a huge part of many London communities and one of the best ways to see a local neighbourhood. In an age where you can order anything online and only need to interact with the person delivering your weekly shop, buying from markets is a different ball game. Not only do stallholders know and love their goods, but the market itself is a fascinating cultural space with its own character, rules and rhythms. These are transient places for social gatherings, meeting friends, seeing familiar faces and exchanging gossip.

Growing up in north London, the capital's markets were a big part of my childhood. We'd stop by Chapel Market and Ridley Road to stock up on fruit, veg and household bits, or go to Columbia Road for a treat. As an alternative teen, markets were an escape for me. I spent hours in Camden Market, buying skull earrings and spiky collars, rummaging around Brick Lane and Spitalfields for 'cool' clothes and going for day trips to Portobello Road with my schoolmates. As an adult, markets are still a huge part of my life, with weekends spent raiding car boot sales, treating myself to expensive kombucha and posh pasta from farmers' markets and scouring street food stalls for my favourite dishes. When my dad died, I knew I had to get the flowers for his funeral from Berwick Street, as we'd spent so much time at that market together. And when my daughter was born at Homerton Hospital, one of the first places she visited was Chatsworth Road Market, just around the corner.

But no matter how long you've spent in London, there are always new spots to discover – as I was delighted to find while researching this book. From fish to flowers, antiques to artichokes, books to bric-a-brac, as well as all the street food imaginable, you could spend every weekend this year visiting a different market in the capital and you'd still have so many more to see... and that's exactly what I recommend you do. Happy rummaging.

Sonya Barber
London, 2025

BEST FOR...

Fresh produce

Borough (no.15) is the big daddy of delicious produce, but there's many more wonderful delights to be found in local markets across the city. Try Marylebone (no.34) for posh bites, Growing Communities (no.47) in Stoke Newington to chat to the growers and Parliament Hill (no.44) for shopping followed by a scenic walk on the Heath.

Unusual antiques

For the ultimate rummage, get up early and head to Sunbury Antiques Market (no.23) for everything from mid-century furniture to dolls' houses. Then there's Grays (no.37) for glinting old watches and one-off jewellery finds, and Alfies (no.39) for 1960s lighting and vintage Christmas baubles.

Vintage threads

Brick Lane Market (no.4) is still the go-to for pre-loved cowboy shirts and French worker jackets, while Camden Passage (no.45) offers up vintage accessories. For more recent hand-me-downs, head to Peckham Car Boot (no.31) for an impressive haul of barely worn Gen Z streetwear.

Local character

Delve into the diversity of Dalston at Ridley Road (no.7), where you'll find Afro-Caribbean fruit and veg, and the best naan breads in London; meet local legends at Deptford (no.29) playing chess, buying old birdcages and eating jerk chicken; and buy handmade soaps, crafts and more from local artisans at Brixton Village (no.18).

Early birds and night owls

If you can get up very early (or stay up very late), you can enter the secret world of chefs, shopkeepers and florists dashing around Billingsgate (no.11) looking for fresh fish, Smithfield (no.12) for the finest cuts and New Covent Garden (no.32) for fresh fruit, vegetables and just-plucked flowers.

Seriously good street food

Lunch at a street food market hits different: steaming boxes of fresh noodles, curries, sushi, wraps, rolls, burgers, buns – whatever cuisine you're craving, you'll find it at these hubs. During the week, if you're lucky enough to be passing by Lower Marsh (no.28), Leather Lane (no.14) or Bloomsbury Farmers' Market (no.13), your belly will thank you. At the weekend, Broadway Market (no.5) always delivers the tasty goods.

Indulging your inner tourist

Camden Market (no.49) is an institution that's well worth a visit to see the old punks and pick up some gothic souvenirs. Quaint Greenwich Market (no.30) has some surprising treasures and Portobello (no.35) is so much more than the set of a Hugh Grant movie, with everything from antiques, vintage clothes and bric-a-brac to freshly made falafels and custard tarts.

SEASONAL MARKETS

CLASSIC CAR BOOT

Victory rolls, berets, tweed, beehives, cowboy hats, leather jackets and blue suede brothel creepers all descend on King's Cross a couple of times a year for this friendly market dedicated to retro subcultures. There are classic cars, vintage clothes from all eras, plenty of vinyl, street food and fantastic people-watching.

classiccarbootsale.co.uk

DIY ART MARKET

See the latest work from some of the capital's coolest creatives at this pop-up market appearing twice a year. This is the place for quirky ceramics, colourful jewellery, fanzines and comics, as well as small sculptures, limited-edition prints and lots of other great gifts for yourself (or others, if you're feeling generous). The Christmas edition is perfect for unique gift shopping, too.

diyartmarket.com

INDEPENDENT LABEL MARKET

Since launching on Berwick Street in 2011, the founders of over 400 independent record labels meet each season to sell their latest releases from market stalls and catch up with pals. There's plenty of beer, band t-shirts and good vibes. Come here to hunt down limited-edition vinyl.

independentlabelmarket.com

SATANIC FLEA MARKET

If Camden Market was reimagined as a hip quarterly pop-up, then this would be the place. Pick up skull candles, pentagram cross stitching, voodoo dolls, gothic jewellery and other celebrations of the dark arts. And for those who prefer bats to baubles, the annual AntiXmas Fayre is a treasure trove of surprising gifts.

instagram.com/satanicfleamarket

CRAFTY FOX MARKET

These crafty foxes have been popping up with markets each Christmas (and a few other times a year) since 2010, showcasing handmade arts and crafts. Pick up gorgeous gifts, plus tongue-in-cheek tree decorations, charmingly rude Christmas cards and other unique treats to pep up the festive season.

craftyfoxmarket.co.uk

ART CAR BOOT FAIR

If Frieze and a car boot sale had a baby, it would be the Art Car Boot Fair. This anarchic bi-annual market has been going since 2004, when it launched with works from Gavin Turk, Abigail Lane, Mat Collishaw, Fiona Banner and Bob & Roberta Smith. Today, you'll find 150 artists selling original works across a wide range of disciplines at slightly more affordable prices. Perfect for picking up a beautiful bargain to start your art collection.

artcarbootfair.com

1

COLUMBIA ROAD FLOWER MARKET

Bloomin' lovely!

Stroll around east London on Sunday and you'll spot an unofficial parade of people laden down with sunflowers, unwieldy cheese plants and bundles of lavender, all slowly streaming away from the hubbub of Columbia Road. This sleepy, picturesque street springs to life early Sunday morning, its stalls bursting with seasonal blooms, trending house plants and outdoor foliage for those lucky enough to have a garden. The air is thick with pollen (hay fever sufferers beware), people and the shouts of traders calling '*threeeeee* bunches for a tenner'. Things can get pretty packed around lunchtime, so go early for prime picks or late to nab some last-minute bargains.

Columbia Road, E2 7RG
Sundays 8am–3pm
Nearest station: Cambridge Heath
columbiaroad.info

2

OLD SPITALFIELDS MARKET

East End institution

A mishmash of architectural styles and old signage gives away the long history of this east London stalwart, which started life as a vibrant fresh fruit and veg trading hub and is now a regenerated shopping hotspot. Skip the mediocre stalls in the new building and head to the refurbished old section for more interesting finds. On Thursdays, it's taken over by an antiques market, filling the covered hall with old maps, vintage Orangina posters, boxes of buttons, Roman coins, fraying flags and lots more homeware and clothes from throughout the last century. There are plenty of strong lunch options, too, but head straight for a Pleasant Lady Chinese jianbing crêpe – the ultimate rummaging reward.

16 Horner Square, E1 6EW
Every day 10am–8pm
Nearest station: Liverpool Street
oldspitalfieldsmarket.com

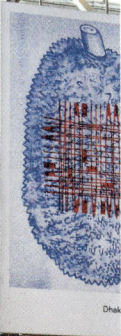

3

NETIL MARKET

Cult food launchpad

This small yard, with its own indie radio station upstairs, has spawned some of the hottest food crazes over the last few years. This is where Bao started selling its fluffy Taiwanese buns (it now has six restaurants across London). Lockdown startup Willy's Pies peddled comfort food here for a few years, and Pockets, the east London falafel sensation, had to move around the corner when it got too popular. At the time of writing, Netil Market hosts brilliant sourdough bagels from Paulie's, serious coffee from Paradox, crisp pizza slices from World Famous Gordos, unctuous ragù from Sugo82 and some rotating pop-ups – but that could all change tomorrow. And that's the beauty of it.

13–23 Westgate Street, E8 3RL
Tuesday to Sunday, 9am–10pm
Nearest station: London Fields
instagram.com/netilmarket

PIZZA BY THE SLICE

WORLD FAMOUS GORDOS

Menu

- MARINARA SUPREME — 3
- NY SLICE — 3.50
- PEPP w/ PAULIE'S EVERYTHING CRUST — 3.75
- CHEF SPECIAL — 4

ICE COLD DRINKS
- PABST — 4 — COLA — 2.50

DIPS —

Koldest Counter
IN TOWN

Open
11 TILL WE AINT

4

BRICK LANE MARKET

Sunday market mainstay

Famous for 24-hour bagel shops, curry houses, vintage clothes and that Monica Ali novel, Brick Lane is a heady mix of influences and cultures. Since the 1700s, it has been home to communities of French Huguenots, Irish, Jewish and Bangladeshi families, now mingling with the hipsters and bankers drifting over from Shoreditch. Sunday has always been market day and today it's still the best (although busiest) time to visit. At the northern end, traders sell antiques, second-hand clothing, books, odds and ends (bargain shoe polish, anyone?). Further down, there are indoor markets in the Old Truman's Brewery selling vintage threads, indie fashion labels, crafty bits and more food, plus weekly pop-ups.

Brick Lane, E1 6PU
Sundays 10am–6pm
Nearest station: Shoreditch High Street

SMO
COFFEE
Espresso
Long Black
Flat White
Latte
Mocha
All available ICED

5

BROADWAY MARKET

Quintessential east London hangout

On a sunny Saturday, it can feel like half of London has descended on this small Hackney thoroughfare. Bikes, buggies, dachshunds and oversized tote bags tangle underfoot as shoppers merrily make their way between Regent's Canal and London Fields. Posh dog snacks, cashmere baby slippers, vintage football books, boob-shaped candles, second-hand kids' clothes, old prints of London, carpets and handmade soap: this is a haven for treats (for yourself and others). There's also food-a-plenty: cheese, breads, brownies, salami, organic vegetables and jars of fiery kimchi to take home, and haggis toasties, bánh mì, jollof rice, samosas and scotch eggs for snacking in the park. Sunday has a similar vibe but with more street food and seating, and less miscellanea.

Broadway Market, E8 4PH
Saturdays 9am–5pm, Sundays 10am–4pm
Nearest station: London Fields
broadwaymarket.co.uk

CARROT
+ ALMOND
LOAF £3.85

NUTELLA
BROWNIES
£3.85

WHITE CHOC
+ RASPBERRY
BROWNIES
£3.85

BANANA
BISCOFF
COOKIE £2.75

LEMON
+RASPBERRY
COOKIE
SANDWICH

6

CHATSWORTH ROAD MARKET

Relaxed Sunday strolling

Chatsworth Road, with its high concentration of hip cafes, delis, boutiques and the poshest Spar supermarket you'll ever visit, was made for mooching – especially on Sundays, when the weekly market springs up. There's enough street food and crafty gifts here to rival Broadway Market, but it's mercifully smaller and more relaxed than its frantic east London neighbour. Decide between freshly wokked pad Thai, Greek souvlaki, jerk chicken or halloumi wraps to be scoffed at one of the makeshift tables. Then it's time for a browse of the other stalls selling flowers, locally made skincare and kids' books, before moseying down to the nearby marshes.

Chatsworth Road, E5 0LH
Sundays 10am–5pm
Nearest station: Homerton
chatsworthroade5.co.uk/market

7

RIDLEY ROAD MARKET

Dalston community hub

There has been a market on Ridley Road since the late 1880s. In the 1950s it was mostly Jewish, in the '60s and '70s it was Caribbean, and then it morphed into a Turkish and Greek market. Today, it's a melange of cultures and a key artery for many Dalston communities, with some of the stalls handed down through multiple generations. Alongside the bowls of fruit, clothes, toiletries, kitchenware, bedding and a wonderful stall devoted entirely to eggs, you can find humongous African land snails (sold alive), bundles of incense, chunks of shea butter and some of the freshest and most delicious naans around from Ararat Bread.

Ridley Road, E8 2NP
Monday to Saturday 9:30am–4pm
Nearest station: Dalston Kingsland
hackney.gov.uk/ridley-road-market

8

WALTHAMSTOW MARKET

A kilometre of useful things

Walthamstow is the proud home of Europe's longest outdoor street market. On and on and on it goes, from Walthamstow Central to St James Street, with stalls selling mounds of fruit, veg and nuts, cleaning supplies, pots and pans, perfumes, luggage, sunglasses, sarcastic doormats, rolls of sequin fabric, kids' fancy dress costumes and baseball caps bearing every slogan imaginable. There's the occasional hipster skirting through holding a succulent, but this is mainly a place to stock up on useful bits and bobs. Be sure to take a pit stop in Market Cafe to admire the impressive display dedicated to Princess Diana over a strong cup of builder's tea.

High Street, E17 7JX
Tuesday to Friday 8am–5pm, Saturdays 8am–5:30pm
Nearest station: Walthamstow Central

9

WOOD STREET INDOOR MARKET

Weird and wonderful time warp

Stepping off the high street into this charming warren of shops feels like being transported to another time and place, a heady combination of a village fête, craft fair, vintage market and tea party. This is a perfect place if you have a fancy dress party coming up: stock up on everything from vintage roller skates and thigh-high boots to sequinned capes and fake eyelashes. There are also antiques shops, mid-mod furniture, records, second-hand books, crystals and incense, hand-knitted baby booties and some paintings of questionable quality, as well as places to get your trainers cleaned or eyebrows threaded. A thoroughly good day out.

98 and 102 Wood Street, E17 3HX
Tuesday to Saturday 10am–5:30pm
Nearest station: Wood Street
woodstreetindoormarket.co.uk

10

LLOYD PARK MARKET

Prams, picnics and pints

Walthamstow's Lloyd Park is parent central. And what do sleep-deprived E17 parents need to get through a weekend? Delicious greasy treats, expensive olives, pastries, strong coffee and maybe even a good pint of craft beer. Well *thank god* for this weekly market, which local families sleepwalk to each Saturday to try the loaded fries, pulled pork sandwiches, arepas and gelato, before settling down next to the sandpit with a flat white (or Bloody Mary). It's all laid out in front of the William Morris Gallery which is definitely worth a look in, too. And if you miss this one, on Sundays there's a similar market run by the same people in Victoria Park.

Forest Road, E17 4PP
Saturdays 10am–4pm
Nearest station: Walthamstow Central
lloydparkmarket.com

TIRAMISU CUBE

£5.75

BISCOFF CUBE

£5.75

£5.75

PRICE LIST
TOMATO CHUTNEY £8
MANGO CHUTNEY £8
MINT + CORIANDER £8
PESTO
CURRY MAYO £8
CHILLI CHICKEN
DRIZZLE £8
CHILLI PRAWN DRIZZLE £8

OFFERS
Buy More, Pay Less
x2 FOR £
x3 FOR £

you're the
chutney to
my samosa

11

BILLINGSGATE FISH MARKET

Fishy business

Rising at 4am to explore a brightly lit warehouse packed with glistening boxes of fish and seafood isn't for the fainthearted. Originally selling a range of produce, Billingsgate became exclusively fishy in the 16th century and has been providing London with the catch of the day ever since (shifting 25,000 tonnes a year). As well as all your standard cods and haddocks, there are crates of eels, wild tiger prawns, giant king crabs and clambering lobsters up for grabs. Reward yourself for the early start with one of the legendary bacon and scallop baps from the cafe, where the walls are covered in old photos of the market and the tables occupied by entertaining characters.

Trafalgar Way, E14 5ST
Tuesday to Saturday, 4am–8:30am
Nearest station: Canary Wharf
cityoflondon.gov.uk

12

SMITHFIELD MARKET

A nocturnal meat and greet

For over 800 years, this iconic central London market has been the city's meaty epicentre. Things come to life at midnight on weekdays, with huge trucks unloading carcasses, workers in blood-splattered overalls and the slap of heavy PVC strip curtains. It might sound a little off-putting, but there's a reason members of the public join the chefs and butchers shopping along Buyers Walk: prime cuts at wholesale prices. Once you've bagged the goods, head over the road for a fry up and strong cuppa at Smithfield Cafe, a 24-hour greasy spoon. Plans have been afoot for several years to move the market to Dagenham, so visit this central London institution while you can.

Smithfield Market, Central Markets, EC1A 9PQ
Weekdays 12am–7am
Nearest stations: Barbican, Farringdon
smithfieldmarket.com

13

BLOOMSBURY FARMERS' MARKET

Scholarly lunchables

Although technically a farmers' market, this weekly pop-up is more of a lunch spot than a place to get groceries. Situated in the shady courtyard between Birkbeck and SOAS universities, there are a few stalls selling organic ingredients – but the mouthwatering array of hot food stalls are the main draw. They set up each Thursday to feed Bloombury's academics, students, librarians and office workers with everything from freshly made Turkish gözleme flatbreads to French buckwheat crêpes. Look out for social enterprise Liberty Kitchen, who work with prisoners to create tasty London-inspired dishes, and Bloomsbury-based artisanal ice cream maker Matter at Hand, churning flavours like Earl Grey and apricot jam.

Torrington Square, WC1E 7HX
Thursdays 9am–2pm
Nearest station: Russell Square
lfm.org.uk/markets/bloomsbury

14

LEATHER LANE MARKET

Hot lunch spot

Oh, the lucky workers of Clerkenwell and Chancery Lane who get to spend their lunch breaks in delicious indecision among these stands. Leather Lane street food market has such an immense number of stalls barbecuing meats, frying falafels, stewing curries and stir-frying noodles that it can be quite overwhelming, especially on an empty stomach. Eat your way through Vietnamese rice bowls, Venezuelan arepas, Korean fried chicken, fresh pasta, Reuben sandwiches (and latkes), Malaysian rendang and Ethiopian stews: follow your gut and you really can't really go wrong.

Leather Lane EC1N 7TJ
Weekdays 10am–3pm
Nearest station: Chancery Lane
instagram.com/leatherlanelondon

INDIAN MENU
CHICKEN DUM BIRYANI
VEG CURRY & RICE
CHICKEN TIKKA & RICE
CHEF SPECIAL
DARASINGH THALI
Drinks

15
BOROUGH MARKET

1,000-year-old food market

You won't find a bigger, bolder and busier food market in the capital than this London Bridge institution. Indeed, it's so famous, that you only need to say the word 'Borough' and people start salivating. Browsing here is a journey of culinary discovery – although it can also be patience-testing on a busy weekend. There's almost too much street food on offer, but you can't go wrong with chorizo and rocket sandwiches from Brindisa. For home cooks, there's plenty to get your apron strings spinning: a plush array of fruit and veg (with a staggering selection of mushroom varieties), imported delicacies from around the world, tried-and-tested kitchenware from Borough Kitchen shop and some amazing wine to accompany your creations.

8 Southwark Street, SE1 1TL
Tuesday to Sunday, 10am–5pm
Nearest station: London Bridge
boroughmarket.org.uk

16

HERNE HILL MARKET

South London foodie fave

For over 20 years, the CCFM (City & Country Farmers' Markets) have been putting on some of London's loveliest weekend markets. These days, they have regular spots in Alexandra Palace, Oval, Stepney, Telegraph Hill and Herne Hill. Each has a slightly different vibe, but the Herne Hill iteration is particularly joyful: set on the quaint pedestrianised street by the station, it has the air of a village fête. This is definitely one for the foodies, stalls groaning with seasonal jams, vegan pastries, oak-smoked garlic, organic chicken, nettle ferments, South African biltong and nuts toasted in saffron and lime – but there's also a handful of other traders selling crafts and clothes to browse on a full stomach.

Railton Road, SE24 0JN
Sundays 10am–4pm
Nearest station: Herne Hill
weareccfm.com

17

TOOTING & BROADWAY MARKETS

Two for the price of one

Tooting is lucky enough to have not one, but *two* tasty indoor markets on the same street. Built in the 1930s, Tooting Market and Broadway Market (no, not that one) are beloved local institutions packed full of international flavours. Eat your way across the continents, bouncing from Mexico to Mauritius, Guyana to Greece. In between the many eateries and bars, you'll find hairdressers, nail salons, locksmiths and a vibrant mix of stalls selling African art, tattoos, dub records, natural skincare, vintage clothes, gold bottles of oud, cheese and wine, fabric, medicinal herbs and old school sweeties stored in glass jars – basically, everything you could ever need.

21–23 and 29 Tooting High Street, SW17
Every day, times vary
Nearest station: Tooting
tootingmarket.com; bmtooting.co.uk

18

BRIXTON MARKETS

Afro-Caribbean essentials and plentiful eats

There's a lot of great mooching to be done in Brixton, with three stellar markets. First, rock down to Electric Avenue – a pedestrianised haven of Caribbean and African produce – then duck into Market Row. Over the last decade, this covered parade has become home to a mix of hip margarita bars, burger and vegan taco joints and political art galleries, as well as votive candle shops, cash-and-carry supermarkets and second-hand stalls. Be sure to pop into The Black Farmer's community-focused deli and cafe before heading over the road to Brixton Village: another indoor arcade of mainly locally run restaurants, shops and stalls. Where to eat can be a tough decision, but you can't go wrong with affordable Thai classics at cash-only Kaosarn.

Electric Avenue, Market Row and Brixton Village, SW9
Every day, times vary
Nearest station: Brixton
brixtonvillage.com

19

BATTERSEA BOOT

Late risers' rummaging spot

Sometimes it can feel like markets, especially car boots, are best suited to morning larks who snaffle all the good stuff before the rest of us have even rolled out of bed. But not Battersea. This obliging car boot opens at a very civilised 1:30pm, making it perfect for anyone for whom the Sunday morning lie-in is sacred. It occupies two playgrounds with varying pitch prices, attracting a real mix of sellers who flog everything from designer dresses to boxes of teacups. But persist with your sifting: previous finds here include a 1980s Janet Jackson tour bomber jacket and a book on cats who paint, so it's well worth the rummage.

Harris Academy, 401 Battersea Park Road, SW11 5AP
Sundays 1:30pm–5pm
Nearest station: Queenstown Road
batterseaboot.com

20

BERMONDSEY ANTIQUE MARKET

Old-school old stuff

Strolling down Bermondsey Street is always a good idea, but never more so than on a Friday morning, when the usually empty square bustles with antiques stalls. This historic market started life in 1855 near Caledonian Road but moved south of the river in 1947 (it's still sometimes known as 'New Caledonian Market'). These days, there are stalls outside selling cameras, costume jewellery and more legit gems, silverware, leather-bound books, birdcages and more. Head inside for a whole wall of teacups and teapots, from bone-china Wedgewood classics to '60s glass sets.

Bermondsey Square, SE1 3UN
Fridays 6am–2pm
Nearest station: London Bridge
bermondseyantiquemarket.co.uk

21

MALTBY STREET MARKET

South London weekend hangout

When this Bermondsey market opened in 2010, it was seen as the cool alternative to nearby food magnet Borough (no.15). Over the years, it's been home to cult London faves, including St. John, and Monty's Deli. These days, those big names are gone, and it's almost as busy with tourists as its London Bridge neighbour, with stalls selling empanadas, raclette with duck fat chips and other hangover-busting comfort nosh. But it's less about the food, more about the vibe. There are atmospheric spots for daytime sangria and G&Ts, former market barrows turned into seating and lots of people lining their stomachs before tackling the Bermondsey Beer Mile.

Ropewalk, Maltby Street, SE1 3PA
Saturdays 10am–5pm, Sundays 11am–4pm
Nearest station: Bermondsey
maltbystreetmarket.co.uk

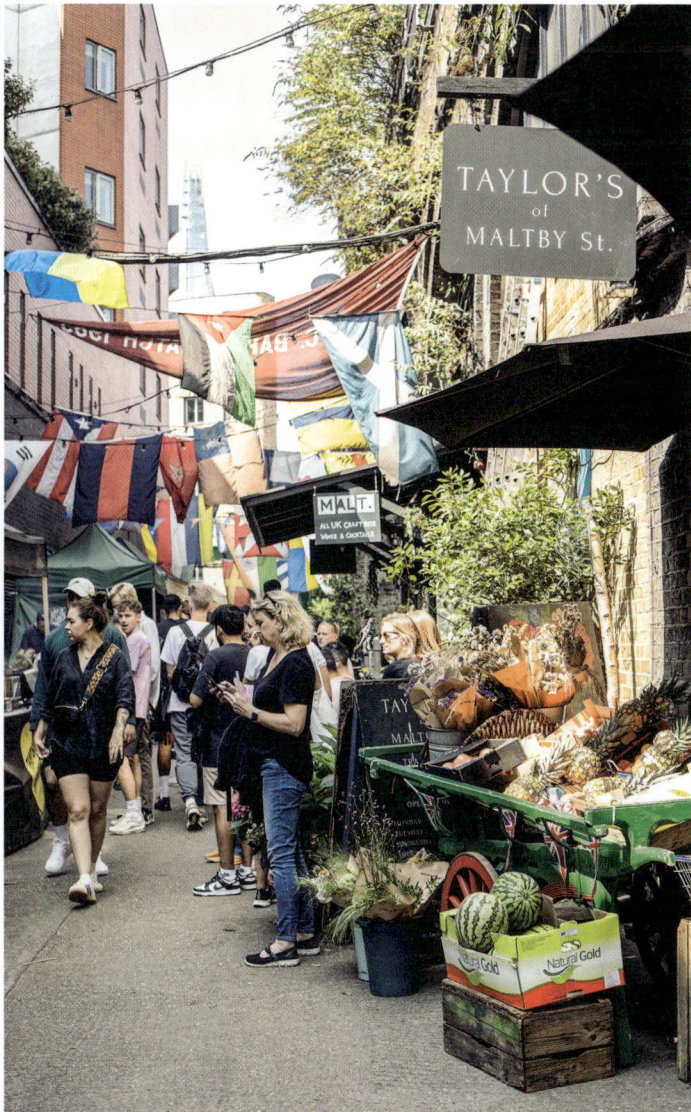

22

SPA TERMINUS

A foodie treasure hunt

Wandering around these industrial railway arches during the week, you'd have little idea that some of London's most prominent independent food purveyors lie behind the shutters. But come on Saturday, and you can fill a tote with goodies direct from the producer. The arches are spread out across various yards, so pick up a map and start exploring. Vendors include Natoora, Kernel Brewery, Monmouth Coffee and Neal's Yard cheeses, but there's also lots of smaller gems to sample, including jams from England Preserves, cordials and drinking vinegars from Gimlet, biodynamic plonk from Dynamic Vines, sweet-smelling granola from Husk and Honey and Ong Ong's wonderful savoury buns.

Dockley Road, SE16 3FJ
Saturdays, times vary
Nearest station: Bermondsey
spa-terminus.co.uk

23

SUNBURY ANTIQUES MARKET

Holy grail of vintage furniture

Okay, so this isn't *technically* in London – but it's only a short train from Waterloo, and it's too epic to miss. Every other Tuesday, this sprawling racecourse turns into one of the UK's largest antiques fairs, filled with stalls trading vintage homewares, furniture, jewellery and so much more. The keen beans and serious collectors arrive early (there's an entrance fee of £5 before 8am), but for the rest of the morning it's everyone from hipsters doing house renovations to locals walking sleepy dogs. Bring cash (and a big bag) or leave disappointed.

Kempton Park Racecourse, Staines Road East,
Sunbury On Thames, TW16 5AQ
Every other Tuesday 6:30am–2pm
Nearest station: Kempton Park
sunburyantiques.com

24

VENN STREET MARKET

Dinner party provisions

Set on a quiet street next to Clapham Common, Venn Street springs to life on Saturday morning with a cheerful array of food and fun. Hangover busting hot bites, including a hog roast or Philly cheesesteak bagels, sit alongside homemade soaps, candles and wool slippers. There's plenty here for the weekly shop, including punnets of soft fruit and boxes of rainbow chard, but what stands out is the great selection of 'picky bits' for a Saturday night of entertaining. Stock up on truffle cheese, olives, salted almonds and classic charcuterie; or for something more unusual, try chewy biltong, hare salami or venison nduja. There are even flowers and decorative gourds to guarantee you are the host with the most.

Venn Street, SW4 0AT
Saturdays 10am–3pm
Nearest station: Clapham Common
vennstreetmarket.co.uk

25

BROCKLEY MARKET

Flowers, ferments and friendly folk

There's a village vibe to this Saturday morning food fair with families and foodies coming from nearby New Cross and Deptford to stock up on provisions and catch up with pals. The basics are all covered – organic vegetables, cheese, meat and fresh fish (including oysters with an array of toppings) – but the market also ticks off a bevy of key food and drink trends: kimchi, krauts and kombucha abound. The hot food selection is plentiful, but save room for Mike & Ollie's legendary flatbreads, filled with mackerel schnitzel or seared Kent pigeon breast with foraged blueberry butter.

Lewisham College Car Park, Lewisham Way, SE4 1UT
Saturdays 10am–2pm
Nearest station: St Johns
brockleymarket.com

PYRENEES
BREBIS

A thermised sheep's
milk cheese made in
Helette, Basque
Pyrenees.

£ 41.70 kg

TOMME DE
SAVOIE

A raw cow's milk
cheese made by
Claude Mercier near
Albertville, Savoie.

£ 29.75 kg

PETIT BLAJA

A raw goat's milk
cheese made by the
Cattenoz family in Midi-
Pyrenees, France.

£ 6.45 half
£ 12.90 whole

26
FLEA LONDON VINTAGE & MAKERS MARKET

Indie shopping

When container city Vinegar Yard first opened just behind London Bridge station in 2019, it felt like a pop-up that would soon fade away. But over half a decade later, it's still going strong, bursting with busy street food stalls and bars. The best bit, though, is the weekend second-hand clothes market. It's charmingly chaotic, smells of incense and gives off an air of 1990s Camden (a good thing, to be clear). Rifle through streetwear, typewriters, cowboy boots, vinyl and football t-shirts – quite the eclectic mix, and nicely juxtaposed with the nearby tables of punters making their way through pints of craft beer and Japanese fried chicken sandos.

Vinegar Yard, St Thomas Street, SE1 3QU
Weekends, times vary
Nearest station: London Bridge
flealondon.com

27

SOUTH BANK
BOOK MARKET

A slice of literary Paris

If you've been to the French capital, chances are you'll have spotted the *bouquinistes*, the vintage booksellers who line the banks of the Seine. Well, this is London's nod to those iconic markets. First opened in 1983 by the controller of the BFI to bring life into the unloved space under Waterloo Bridge, this daily market is still a favourite among anyone taking a romantic amble along the river or killing time before a cultural outing at the Southbank Centre. It's a random hodgepodge of Penguin Classics, leatherbound 'ye olde' books and semi-collectable comics, but you'll usually find something that catches your eye.

Under Waterloo Bridge, SE1 8TX
Every day 10am–5:30pm
Nearest station: Waterloo

28

LOWER MARSH MARKET

Waterloo street food stop-off

There's been a market on this small side street behind Waterloo Station since the 1800s. Once famed as the longest street market in the UK, today's iteration is significantly smaller – but what it lacks in length, it makes up for in enthusiasm. This is one of the best spots in the area for a well-priced lunch, with cohorts of rail, theatre and office workers gossiping in the queues for steaming boxes of Nigerian stew, Thai curry, Tibetan momos and Korean bibimbap. As well as filling bellies, the market also has some equally nourishing community events, including lunchtime gardening clubs, cycle surgeries, film screenings and even a Christmas performance.

Lower Marsh, SE1 7RJ
Weekdays 11am–3pm
Nearest station: Waterloo
lowermarshmarket.com

29

DEPTFORD MARKETS

A mass of trash and treasure

Lucky old Deptford has two good markets, one that spans most of Deptford High Street and a smaller one outside The Albany theatre. While the first offers fruit and veg, boxes of biscuits, "Chanel" tea towels and cheap cosmetics, the second one is the real doozy – an astounding collection of bric-a-brac. Bikes, old computers, roller skates, punching bags, pianos, record players, hedge trimmers and fish tanks – it's messy, chaotic and completely *un*curated, so you can unearth some seriously cool stuff if you look hard enough. Local families and Goldsmiths art students scour the piles of junk while stallholders play chess. One of the most unusual rummaging spots in town.

Deptford High Street, Douglas Way, SE8 4BX
Wednesdays, Fridays and Saturdays 9am–5:30pm
Nearest station: Deptford

30
GREENWICH MARKET

Loveable tourist trap

There's no getting around it – this is a seriously touristy market. And it's no wonder, considering how close it is to the Cutty Sark, Royal Observatory and National Maritime Museum. Like a twee Camden Market, there are Union Jack-patterned trinkets and phone box keyrings aplenty, but there's still an indie feel beyond the tourist tat, with stallholders selling handmade goods from zingy acrylic earrings to knitted kids' clothes. Some of the best stuff here is actually around the edges of the stalls: a zero-waste shop, Korean beauty products and an old-school sweet store. Go with kids in tow, friends visiting from out of town or if you need a present for a friend with particularly kitsch taste.

Greenwich Market, SE10 9HZ
Every day 10am–5:30pm
Nearest station: Cutty Sark
greenwichmarket.london

31

PECKHAM CARBOOT

Hipster hotspot

Each Sunday morning, a queue of eager bargain hunters snakes around Lidl supermarket. 'Everything will be gone by the time we get there!' worries the fashionable youth waiting in line behind me. But despite being impressively popular, there's enough booty for everyone, with two playgrounds packed with stalls. There's streetwear, sheepskin coats, sunflower plants, John Steinbeck novels, dream catchers and rails of clothes labelled for 'goths, gays, skaters'. Fair warning: it's overwhelming and will easily take up a whole morning. Swing by the coffee cart to keep you buzzing and pick up a Peckham Carboot tote bag to show how cool you are.

Bellenden Road, SE15 5DZ
Every other Sunday 10am–2pm
Nearest station: Peckham Rye
peckhamcarboot.com

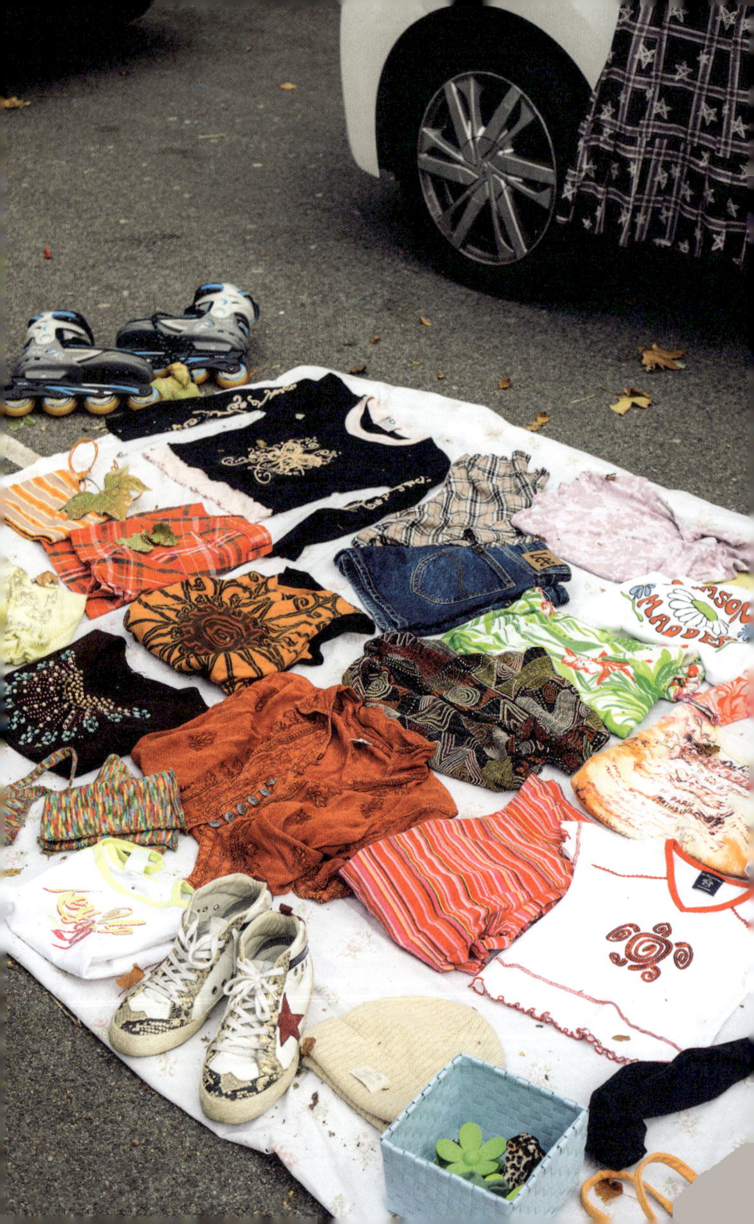

32

NEW COVENT GARDEN MARKET

Fruit, veg and flowers overflowing

This is the heavyweight of London wholesale markets – the largest in the UK, with 32 acres of fruit, veg, flowers and more sold every night. There's a lot going on here, so plan your visit carefully. Come between 2am and 5am to inspect boxes of well-priced passion fruits, stripey tomatoes, giant watermelons and fresh herbs; if it's grown somewhere in the world, you can find it here. At 4am, flowers are unloaded, the hall filled with more blooms, leafy foliage and plants than you've ever laid eyes on. The sellers know their stuff, so whether you're looking for bespoke wedding bouquets at wholesale prices, or just want a living room's worth of sunflowers, this is the place.

New Covent Garden Market, sw8 5bh
Monday to Saturday, times vary
Nearest station: Battersea Power Station
newcoventgardenmarket.com

Caution
Slippery floor
surface

33

CHISWICK FLOWER MARKET

West London in bloom

We all know about Columbia Road (no.1), but this lovely little flower market is a better-kept secret. On the first weekend of the month, a friendly celebration of flowers and foliage springs up on Old Market Place, selling everything from freshly cut blooms to houseplants and succulents. This is the place to chat green ideas and load up on bulbs and seeds from previous Chelsea Flower Show RHS winners (a.k.a. the UK's finest gardeners). Once you're all flowered out, look for the adjacent pop-up markets, including the vegan market for meat-free treats and the Open Art Spaces for cool arts and crafts.

Chiswick High Road, w4 2DR
First Sunday of the month 9am–3:30pm
Nearest station: Turnham Green
chiswickflowermarket.com

34

MARYLEBONE FARMERS' MARKET

Chic shoppers galore

There's a bounty of farmers' markets in London, but none quite so classy as Marylebone. Never-mind rare vegetable varieties; you can buy *entire crates* of oysters. Each Sunday, this buzzing market proffers a wealth of high-end groceries, from bags of edible flowers to goat's cheese roulades. And it's not only the produce that's top notch; there are also some impressively posh ready meals to fill your fridge (ayurvedic curries, anyone?). Once the shopping has been done, join the merry queues for truffled scallop sandwiches, artisan crumpets or sizzling organic sausage baps to devour on a bench in Paddington Street Gardens.

St Vincent Street, W1U 4DF
Sundays 10am–2pm
Nearest station: Marylebone
lfm.org.uk/markets/marylebone

Blackberry
Frangipane
£8.50

Pear
Frangipane
£8.50

Chestnut
Mushroom Quiche
£7.00 or
2 for £13

Roast Veg
Quiche
£7.00 or
2 for £13

Apple Crumble
£3.75

Apple + Blackberry
Crumble
£3.75

Quiche
Lorr
£7.0
2 for

35

PORTOBELLO ROAD MARKET

West London legend

Portobello Road Market is a lot of things to a lot of people. During the week, there are stalls selling fruit and veg, tacky Big Ben t-shirts and bric-a-brac. These are the quieter days when you'll see locals doing their weekly shops and tourists looking for Hugh Grant and Julia Roberts. Friday is the best day for vintage fashion and furniture, with stacks of French workers' jackets, sequinned dresses and '80s band t-shirts under the Westway flyover and towards Golborne Road. The offering is in full swing on Saturdays, with the antiques market selling everything from china chamber pots to jewellery new and old. Reward yourself after a rummage with a gooey custard tart from Lisboa Patisserie.

Portobello Road, W11 1LJ
Monday to Saturday, times vary
Nearest station: Ladbrook Grove
portobelloroad.co.uk

NOW SHOWING

JOKER

HONEST

NOTTING
HILLGATE

KENSINGTON AND CHELSEA
LONDON

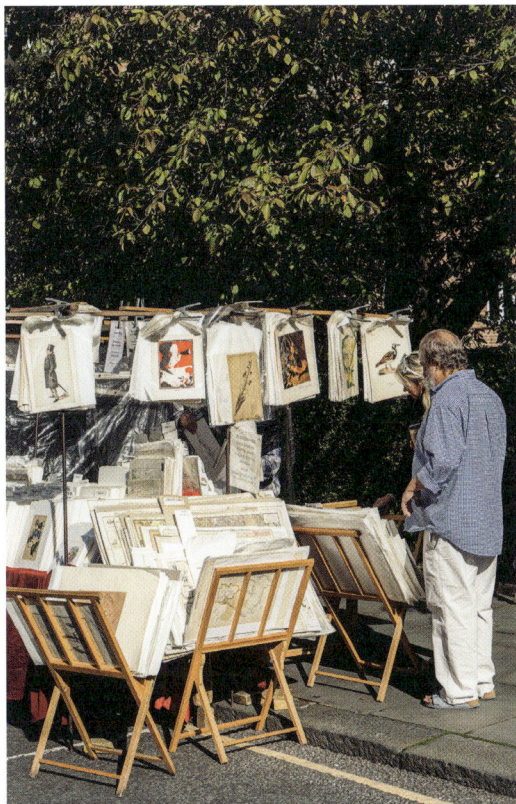

36

BERWICK STREET MARKET

Historic Soho lunch spot

It might look like just another street food spot, but this Soho strip is actually one of London's oldest markets, home to stalls since 1778. Westminster Council threatened to sell the land to a private landlord in 2016, but the traders won the battle to remain independent, keeping a bit of 'old' Soho alive. Today, it's mostly food trucks, serving up great grub at speed: burgers, fragrant curries, fried noodles, salads and unmissable falafel wraps. There's still a smattering of the market's former self as a practical shopping destination, with a few stalls selling fruit and veg, responsibly sourced milk, eggs and blooms, all priced reasonably (for Soho, anyway).

Berwick Street, W1F 0PH
Monday to Saturday 8am–6pm
Nearest station: Piccadilly Circus

37

GRAYS ANTIQUE MARKET

A magpie's dream

The hushed tones of Grays sellers whispering antiques-world gossip feels a million miles away from the brash chaos of nearby Oxford Street. This ornate, Grade II-listed building houses almost 100 dealers of jewellery, antiques, watches and random collectables – and these guys are serious about their wares. Expectant stallholders will advise you on everything from glittering opals and diamonds to ceramic sweetcorn teapots. Sixteenth-century Chinese Ming Dynasty vases jostle for space among swan ice buckets, military paraphernalia, clocks, hip flasks and cases of small gold charms – something for everyone (if you've got the pocket money).

58 Davies Street, London W1K 5LP
Weekdays 10am–6pm
Nearest station: Bond Street
graysantiques.com

38

CHISWICK CHEESE MARKET

Monthly fromage fest

Legend has it that Chiswick was once called Cheesewick, which makes this an apt spot for the capital's only fromage fair. Started in 2020 by a bunch of local foodies, it was originally intended to support the country's independent cheese producers during the pandemic, but has since turned into a monthly dairy-lovers dream. With over 200 fromages on offer, this truly is a cheesy paradise: mozzarella and burrata made in west London (Stanley Tucci-approved), wheels of parmesan to make Samuel Pepys blush and surprisingly realistic vegan cheeses, plus plenty of tasting opportunities. There are also toasties, mac 'n' cheese and Basque cheesecake to scoff while you shop.

Chiswick High Road, w4 2DR
Third Sunday of the month 9:30am–3pm
Nearest station: Turnham Green
chiswickcheesemarket.uk

39

ALFIES ANTIQUE MARKET

A labyrinth of loot

Whatever time of year you visit Alfies, you'll be welcomed by a Christmas tree bedecked in vintage decorations (including those iconic 1950s pickle-shaped glass baubles). Operating for over 40 years, this is a delightfully confusing maze of objects, clothes and accessories spanning centuries and continents, culminating in a surreal mirrored fishpond and large hammerhead shark sculpture at the centre. Upstairs is retro homeware, lampshades and a pink cocoon of 1950s glamour adorned with furs and dusty bottles of Chanel; persist further still and you'll reach the cheery rooftop cafe serving eggs Benedict and wine.

13–25 Church Street, NW8 8DT
Tuesday to Saturday 10am–6pm
Nearest station: Marylebone
alfiesantiques.com

40

SHEPHERD'S BUSH MARKET

Fabric, falafels and exotic fruit

Shepherd's Bush is such a culturally significant market that it has even lent its name to a tube station. There has been a trading spot along this railway line since 1914, and despite the ongoing threat of redevelopment, it's still an essential part of the community. Smells of incense mingle with frying food, and locals chat while doing their weekly shop. There are also copious fabric and haberdashery shops, plus regular screen-printing workshops held in one of the market arches. The eateries here serve a range of delicious lunches, from Japanese rice balls to Ethiopian stews, but if you're *really* hungry, head to Mr Falafel – their XL wrap is enough for two.

Uxbridge Road, W12 8DF
Monday to Saturday 9am–6pm
Nearest station: Shepherd's Bush Market
shepherdsbushmarket.org

41

DUKE OF YORK SQUARE FINE FOOD MARKET

Posh nosh, darling

You'd expect a food market on the King's Road to be luxe, but the cocktail bar that greets you – stocked with mini champagne bottles – is almost comically decadent. Curated by swanky supermarket Partridges, the food stalls lining the square outside the Saatchi gallery are *fancy*: confit duck sandwiches, truffled scallops served in their shell and trays of briny oysters. But among the lavish treats and produce, there's also a stellar range of street food stalls selling somewhat more affordable grub from around the world. Come hungry, bring a rug (or buy an overpriced one here) and settle down on the lawn for a first-class feast.

80 Duke of York Square, SW3 4LY
Saturdays 8am–4pm
Nearest station: Sloane Square
dukeofyorksquare.com

42

PRINCESS MAY
CAR BOOT SALE

Rummagers' paradise

Hackney's only car boot is exactly as you'd imagine: hungover hipsters flogging their last season's Ganni dresses, families offloading old toys, vintage collectors selling their curiosities and regulars who bag the same spot every week. It's a joyful hodgepodge of items, where you might find an old Alexander McQueen outfit for a tenner and a Taschen photography book for a quid – or come home with a ceramic hot water bottle and all the Twilight films on DVD and wonder what you were thinking. Whatever treasures you unearth, it's always worth the entry fee (just £1 after 9am) – especially for the cheap sausage sandwiches sold in the corner of the schoolyard.

Princess May School, N16 8DF
Weekends 7:30am–2pm
Nearest station: Dalston Kingsland

BELLINI
MATCH
EDWARD
NICK CARTER
Picture Show
NICK CARTER
THE SNAKE
Motor Cycle News
NICK CARTER
LITERARY WORLD
THE NATION'S BEST PICTURES
NATION'S
FILM REVIEW

43

CHAPEL MARKET

Islington stalwart

This street has been home to a market for over 150 years, furnishing the people of Islington with cheap fruit and veg, toys, toiletries and a monkey who used to sit on your shoulder (true story). Today, there's a smattering of street food stalls, a cheese stand where you can order freshly made sandwiches for under a fiver, oysters, house plants and a whole stall dedicated to ceramic seconds, including rather nice Habitat tableware and William Morris mugs. Plus, there's the brilliantly bonkers all-you-can-eat Indian Veg restaurant, its walls lined with plant-based propaganda. On Sunday, the vibe shifts a little more upmarket, as the last block offers a vegan feminist bakery, bags of posh salad leaves and punnets of seasonal fruit.

Chapel Market, N1 9EW
Tuesday to Sunday, times vary
Nearest station: Angel
instagram.com/chapelmarketn1

44

PARLIAMENT HILL FARMERS' MARKET

Heath-side provisions

To find this popular farmers' market, all you need to do is follow the dog walkers with bunches of carrots and leeks poking out of their tote bags, and kids sipping bottles of raw milk. Some Saturday mornings it can feel like the whole of north London is here, loading up on knobbly cucumbers, fresh pasta, seasonal blooms and bone broth. Not only is there an impressive selection of organic produce, cheese, salty seafood and free-range meat, but there are also plenty of hot food options, whether you fancy posh sausages or vegan gyoza dunked in hot dipping sauce.

William Ellis School, off Highgate Road, NW5 1RN
Saturdays 10am–2pm
Nearest station: Gospel Oak
lfm.org.uk/markets/parliament-hill

45

CAMDEN PASSAGE MARKET

Antiques meet brunch

You could easily walk through Angel and have no clue that just one road back from the cacophony of Upper Street is a pedestrianised passage full of treasures. Most days, it's a pleasant place for a stroll, with alfresco cafe tables, an inexplicably long queue for The Breakfast Club and lots of cute independent shops. But on Wednesdays and Saturdays, stalls appear and shutters spring up, turning this street into an antiques hub. Explore Pierrepont Arcade to find colourful costume jewellery, berets, gloves and trilby hats, alongside records, Charles and Diana memorabilia, lavish birdcages and intricate botanical prints. Look out for the stall completely laden with ornate china teacups.

Camden Passage, N1 8EA
Wednesdays and Saturdays 9am–6pm
Nearest station: Angel
camdenpassageislington.co.uk

46

HOXTON STREET MARKET

A slice of the East End

Given its proximity to Shoreditch, there's surprisingly little hipsterfication of this weekly market. Follow the smell of jerk wafting from the Caribbean food van and secure a saltfish patty to fuel your browsing. You could easily buy a whole outfit for a tenner here, with sportswear, evening gowns, shoes, handbags, £1 sunglasses and dubiously cheap "designer" gear on offer. Stop at mother-and-daughter-run PKs Seafood stall for a scallop and bacon bap, a pot of cockles or some freshly peeled prawns; or if you want to go even more old-school, one of London's last remaining pie-and-mash shops, F. Cooke, serves up traditional pies with liquor and jellied or stewed eels all Saturday.

Hoxton Street, N1 6SH
Saturdays 9am–4pm
Nearest station: Hoxton
instagram.com/hoxtonstmarket

47

GROWING COMMUNITIES FARMERS' MARKET

Superior produce selection

Not all farmers' markets are created equal: this Stoke Newington stalwart is the fairest of them all. Striving to build a more sustainable, ethical food system, Growing Communities offers volunteering opportunities, veg boxes and (of course) an excellent array of produce sourced from organic and biodynamic farms in and around London. Pick up Dagenham aubergines, gourmet mushrooms from Essex, Walthamstow honey, Kent cherries and salad leaves from Hackney. There's a bounty of exciting seasonal fruit and veg, good cheese and homemade pickles, plus a wooden playground to entertain small ones while you chill with a kombucha.

St Paul's Church, N16 7UE
Saturdays 10am–2:30pm
Nearest station: Rectory Road
growingcommunities.org/market

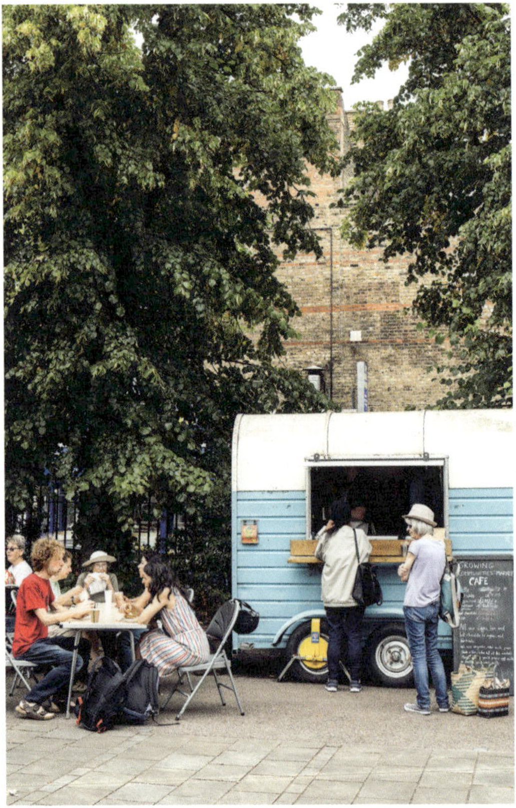
GROWING
CAFE

48

HACKNEY FLEA MARKET

Roving second-hand emporium

Don't let the name fool you. This roving market isn't just in Hackney – it pops up across London – and it's more of a classy collectors' fair than a rummagers' flea. This is the place to find gorgeous vintage furniture, homewares and clothes from yesteryear. There's a wealth of mid-century teak sideboards, garish orange and brown '70s kitchenware, neon signs and kooky lamps, bold-coloured enamel jugs, rocking chairs and rugs to suit every home. Plus, second-hand garms, with patch-covered denim jackets and cowboy boots to help you look the part.

73a Stoke Newington Church Street, N16 0AS
Other locations: see website
Times vary
hackneyfleamarket.com

49

CAMDEN MARKET

The spiritual home of angsty teens

No book on London's markets would be complete without Camden. It's been cleaned up in recent years, but this maze of interlinked markets has a grimy countercultural heritage that dates back to the '70s. Punks with multicoloured mohicans hang around on the bridge (now charging £2 for a photo), rave shop Cyberdog blasts techno and the smells of incense and fried food fill the air. Anyone who had an alt teen phase will be thrilled by leather-studded chokers, corsets and Nirvana T-shirts. And among the many stands and arches of tourist tat, there are some genuinely decent vintage shops, including an archive of historical frames at General Eyewear. Just don't go at the weekend if you can possibly help it.

Camden Lock Place, NW1 8AF
Every day, times vary
Nearest station: Camden Road
camdenmarket.com

50

STROUD GREEN MARKET

Community hub

Passionate local Ed May set up this joyful produce market in 2017 after noticing the lack of fresh 'real' food fairs in the area. Every Sunday since then, Stroud Green Primary School's playground has been bustling with organic meat, eggs and wild mushrooms, as well as locally made sourdough, Haringey honey and Hampstead cheese. On the first Sunday of each month, the market hosts a delightful 'Long Table Lunch' courtesy of Communi Table, where delicious seasonal produce is turned into a three-course veggie extravaganza, enjoyed communally with neighbours. A true locals' market if ever there was one.

Stroud Green School, Perth Road N4 3HB
Sundays 10am–2:30pm
Nearest station: Finsbury Park
stroudgreenmarket.com

CONTRIBUTORS

Sonya Barber is a freelance travel, food and culture writer. She is a former editor at *Time Out London* and *Condé Nast Traveller* and the author of four Opinionated Guides by Hoxton Mini Press. Thanks to researching this book, she now has an addiction to farmers' market kombucha.

Hoxton Mini Press is a small indie publisher based in east London. We make books about London (and beyond) with a dedication to lovely, sustainable production and brilliant photography. When we started the company, people told us 'print was dead'; we wanted to prove them wrong. Books are no longer just about information but objects in their own right: things to collect and own and inspire. We are an environmentally conscious publisher, committed to offsetting our carbon footprint. This book, for instance, is 100 per cent carbon compensated, with offset purchased from Stand for Trees.

An Opinionated Guide to
London Markets

First edition, first printing

Published in 2025 by Hoxton Mini Press,
London. Copyright © Hoxton Mini Press
2025. All rights reserved.

Text by Sonya Barber.
Editing by Florence Ward.
Design and production by Dom Grant.
Proofreading by Zoë Jellicoe.
With thanks to Matthew Young for
initial series design.

Please note: we recommend checking the
websites listed for each entry before you
visit for the latest information on price,
opening times and pre-booking
requirements.

A CIP catalogue record for this book is
available from the British Library.

ISBN: 978-1-914314-76-6

Printed and bound by OZGraf, Poland

Hoxton Mini Press is an environmentally
conscious publisher, committed to
offsetting our carbon footprint. This book
is 100 per cent carbon compensated, with
offset purchased from Stand For Trees.

Every time you order from our website, we
plant a tree: www.hoxtonminipress.com

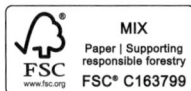

MIX
Paper | Supporting
responsible forestry
FSC
www.fsc.org
FSC® C163799

Selected opinionated guides in the series:

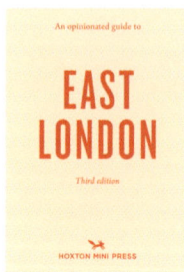

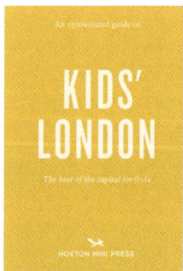

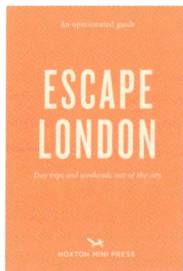

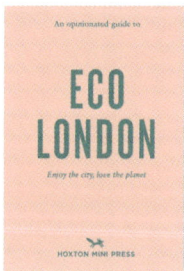

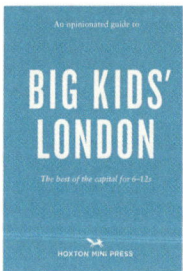

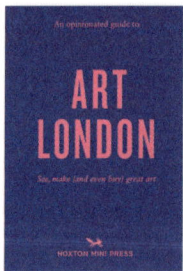

An opinionated guide to
EAST LONDON
Third edition
HOXTON MINI PRESS

An opinionated guide to
LONDON
HOXTON MINI PRESS

An opinionated guide to
LONDON GREEN SPACES
HOXTON MINI PRESS

An opinionated guide to
LONDON FOOD
The places you have to try
HOXTON MINI PRESS

An opinionated guide to
KIDS' LONDON
The best of the capital for 0–5s
HOXTON MINI PRESS

An opinionated guide
ESCAPE LONDON
Day trips and weekends out of the city
HOXTON MINI PRESS

An opinionated guide to
ECO LONDON
Enjoy the city, love the planet
HOXTON MINI PRESS

An opinionated guide to
BIG KIDS' LONDON
The best of the capital for 6–12s
HOXTON MINI PRESS

An opinionated guide to
ART LONDON
See, make (and even buy) great art
HOXTON MINI PRESS

For more go to www.hoxtonminipress.com

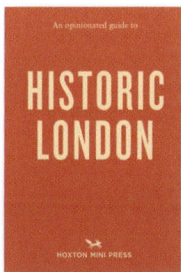

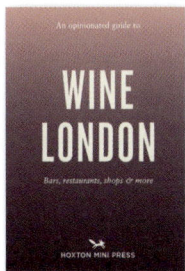

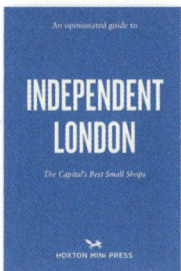

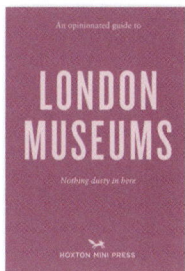

An opinionated guide to
LONDON CANALS
Nature, food and fun along the city's waterways
HOXTON MINI PRESS

An opinionated guide to
FREE LONDON
Enjoy the capital without the cash
HOXTON MINI PRESS

An opinionated guide to
DESIGN LONDON
Galleries, shops, museums & more
HOXTON MINI PRESS

An opinionated guide to
LONDON ARCHITECTURE
HOXTON MINI PRESS

An opinionated guide to
HISTORIC LONDON
HOXTON MINI PRESS

An opinionated guide to
LONDON BOOKSHOPS
HOXTON MINI PRESS

An opinionated guide to
WINE LONDON
Bars, restaurants, shops & more
HOXTON MINI PRESS

An opinionated guide to
INDEPENDENT LONDON
The Capital's Best Small Shops
HOXTON MINI PRESS

An opinionated guide to
LONDON MUSEUMS
Nothing dusty in here
HOXTON MINI PRESS

INDEX